MW01075618

SPIRITUAL DISCIPLINES

# REFLECTION & CONFESSION

BIBLE STUDIES

## Jan Johnson

6 STUDIES WITH NOTES FOR LEADERS

Inter-Varsity Press
Nottingham, England

IVP Connect
An imprint of InterVarsity Press
Downers Grove, Illinois

InterVarsity Press, USA
P.O. Box 1400, Downers Grove, IL 60515-1426, USA
World Wide Web: www.ivpress.com
Email: email@ivpress.com

Inter-Varsity Press, England
Norton Street, Nottingham NG7 3HR, England
World Wide Web: www.ivpbooks.com
Email: ivp@ivpbooks.com

InterVarsity Press® is the book-publishing division of InterVarsity Christian Fellowship/USA®, a student movement active on campus at hundreds of universities, colleges and schools of nursing in the United States of America, and a member movement of the International Fellowship of Evangelical Students. For information about local and regional activities, write Public Relations Dept., InterVarsity Christian Fellowship/USA, 6400 Schroeder Rd., P.O. Box 7895, Madison, WI 53707-7895, or visit the IVCF website at <www.intervarsity.org>.

Inter-Varsity Press, England, is closely linked with the Universities and Colleges Christian Fellowship (formerly the Inter-Varsity Fellowship), a student movement linking Christian Unions in universities and colleges throughout the United Kingdom and the Republic of Ireland, and a member movement of the International Fellowship of Evangelical Students. For information about local and national activities write to UCCF, 38 De Montfort Street, Leicester LE1 7GP, email them at email@uccf.org.uk or visit the UCCF website at www.uccf.org.uk.

All Scripture quotations, unless otherwise indicated, are taken from the Holy Bible, New International Version®. NIV®. Copyright ©1973, 1978, 1984 by International Bible Society. Used by permission of Zondervan Publishing House. All rights reserved. Distributed in the U.K. by permission of Hodder and Stoughton Ltd. All rights reserved. "NIV" is a registered trademark of International Bible Society. UK trademark number 1448790.

Cover design: Cindy Kiple

Cover and interior image: Digital Vision

U.S. ISBN 978-0-8308-2093-1

U.K. ISBN 978-0-85111-694-5

Printed in the United States of America ∞

| P | 19 | 18 | 17 | 16 | 15 | 14 | 13 | 12 | 11 | 10 | 9 | 8 | 7 | 6 | 5 | 4 |
| Y | 22 | 21 | 20 | 19 | 18 | 17 | 16 | 15 | 14 | 13 | 12 | 11 | 10 | | | | |

# CONTENTS

# INTRODUCING
## *Reflection & Confession*

Have you ever wondered how God changes people? Maybe it seems as if old habits never change no matter how hard you try. Maybe you've become discouraged with your lack of growth into Christlikeness. You know that you are forgiven through Jesus' suffering on the cross, and you realize that you are totally accepted by God on that basis. This is wonderful. And yet your desire to live in a way that pleases God somehow constantly falls short of the mark.

God desires to transform our souls. This transformation occurs as we recognize that God created us to live in an interactive relationship with the Trinity. Our task is not to transform ourselves, but to stay connected with God in as much of life as possible. As we pay attention to the nudges of the Holy Spirit, we become disciples of Christ. Our task is to do the connecting, while God does the perfecting.

As we connect with God, we gradually begin acting more like Christ. We become more likely to weep over our enemies instead of discrediting them. We're more likely to give up power instead of taking control. We're more likely to point out another's successes rather than grab the credit. Connecting with God changes us on the inside, and we slowly become the tenderhearted, conscientious people our families always wished we'd become. This transformation of our souls through the work of the Holy Spirit results in "Christ in you, the hope of glory" (Colossians 1:27).

God does in us what we cannot do by being good. Trying to be good generally makes us obnoxious because it's so obvious that we're only trying. The goodness doesn't come from within ourselves. When we do succeed at being good, we subtly look down on those who don't do as well. When we don't succeed, we beat ourselves up and despair over our lack of spirituality. Either way, we remain focused on self instead of on setting our hearts on things above.

Connecting with God, then, is important. But what does connecting with God look like? Through the work of the Holy Spirit, we copy Jesus in behind-the-scenes, everyday activities he did to connect with God. As we let these activities become habits, we slowly become "trained" to have the heart of Christ and behave as he did. These activities are spiritual disciplines, also called spiritual exercises or strategies.

## How Spiritual Disciplines Work

We connect with God through spiritual disciplines or exercises. Reflection and confession, the topics of these Bible studies, are two of them. Other disciplines include solitude, silence, Bible study, Scripture meditation, worship, celebration, prayer, listening, service, secrecy, fasting, simplicity, community and submission. These exercises are studied in the other Spiritual Disciplines Bible Studies. Still other disciplines can be used, some of which are written about in the classics of the faith and others God will show you. Henri Nouwen said that a spiritual discipline is anything that helps us practice "how to become attentive to that small voice and willing to respond when we hear it."*

---

*Sources for quoted material can be found at the end of the guide.

How do spiritual disciplines help us connect with God?

- They build our relationship with God as we acquaint ourselves with the ways of God. (It's possible, of course, to do these disciplines in a legalistic way and never bond with Christ.)

- They build our trust in Christ. Some of the disciplines are uncomfortable. You have to go out on a limb. You try fasting, and you don't die. You serve someone, and it turns out to be fun and enriching.

- They force us to make "little decisions" that multiply. Your little decision to abstain from watching a television show helps you to deny yourself and love others in all sorts of ways.

- They reorganize our impulses so that obedience is more natural. For example, if you have a spiritual discipline of practicing the presence of God, you may learn to automatically pray the breath prayer "into thy hands" when someone opposes you. Without your realizing it, your opponent is no longer an adversary, but a person God is dealing with or perhaps even speaking through in some way.

- They help us eventually behave like Christ—but this is by God's miraculous work, not our direct effort.

- They teach us to trust that God will do the work in our inner being through the power of the Spirit (Ephesians 3:16). Your spirituality is not about you; it's the work of God in you. You get to cooperate in God's "family business" of transforming the world.

## How We Get Spiritual Disciplines Wrong

Spiritual exercises must be done with the goal of connecting, not for any sake of their own or any desire to check them off a list of "to do" items. If you read your Bible just to get it done, or because you've heard this will help you have a better day, you'll be anxious to complete the Bible study questions or to get to the bottom of the page of today's reading. But if your goal in Bible reading is to connect with God, you may pause whenever you sense God speaking to you. You'll stop and meditate on it. You may pray certain phrases back to God, indicating your needs or your wishes or your questions. You may choose to read that passage day after day for a month because God keeps using it to speak to you.

After such a session, you will have a stronger desire to connect with God. That "little choice" you made to connect will leave you slightly different for life.

The exercise or discipline is beneficial because it helps you practice connecting with God. If you want to play the piano well or swing a tennis racket well, you have to practice certain exercises over and over. Good baseball players train behind the scenes by practicing their batting day after day, with no crowds watching.[*] That's what spiritual disciplines or exercises are about. If you can hear God in fasting and simplicity, you'll more likely hear God in a board meeting or an altercation with a recalcitrant teen when passions run high. In life with God, we get good at connecting on an everyday basis by devoting time to developing the skills needed.

## The Disciplines of Reflection and Confession

The spiritual exercises of reflection and confession don't sound as upbeat as worship and celebration or as intimate as prayer and listening. Yet when they are rightly understood, learned and practiced, these disciplines become a valuable part of our conversation with God that enlivens our days and brightens our souls.

Perhaps you need this study to help you let go of the idea that reflect-

---

[*]This comparison originated from and is expanded in Dallas Willard, *The Spirit of the Disciplines* (San Francisco: Harper & Row, 1988), p. 3.

ing on your mistakes and owning up to them is discouraging. For to-day's performance-driven Christians, self-examination might as well be self-annihilation. But such thinking is part of the murky distortion that God is upset with you unless you do everything right and that your spirituality is really about *you*. Quite the contrary: we realize that as disciples of Jesus we are "dust" and that God delights in shaping us into new creations. Faith is centered not on our performance but on the constant choice of God to love us, accept us and transform us into creatures who know how to love. Reflection and confession are some of the many ways God shows us the way forward—if we're willing to look.

Scripture is clear that confessing sins and praying with others is a positive move in the healing process (James 5:16). The never-giving-up love of God, who doesn't keep a record of wrongs, far outweighs our sins. Our brutal honesty is met by God's gritty acceptance, and the result is that we are bonded to the heart of God.

Because God's goodness and love are foundational to reflection and confession, this series begins with a session on the compassionate nature of God, who is not shocked by our sin. Instead of getting mad, God wants to forgive and heal. After this foundational study, we move into reflection, confessing to God and confessing to others. Then we look at practical methods: the classic prayer of examen (examining both our conscience and our daily consciousness of God) and journaling.

## How Do These Studies Work?

The studies in this guide examine examples, attitudes and methods of these disciplines in our lives. Each session includes several elements.

**Turning Toward God** presents discussion or reflection questions and exercises to draw us into the topic at hand.

**Hearing God Through the Word** draws us into a study of a related passage of Scripture with questions that connect it to life and invite us to reflect on what God is saying.

*Transformation Exercises* are activities or thoughts to experiment with in order to experience the spiritual exercise studied. At the end of the study, look at these exercises and choose the one that fits you best, according to your personality or your current needs. Think of a time to try it on your own, and report back to the group the following week.

Perhaps you'll read the exercise and think it's too elementary or too difficult for you. Adapt it as needed. Or maybe you think you can guess what you'll experience, so you don't have to do it. The point is to experience it. Go ahead and try.

## Using These Studies in Retreats

These studies work well for an individual taking a personal retreat. Simply do the studies at your own pace, and do not rush them. Allow enough time to do the transformation exercises as well. Don't feel you have to do all the studies. In fact, you may wish to focus only on one discipline and use only those studies.

A group wishing to explore certain disciplines can also use one of these studies the same way. Be sure to allow time for participants to do the transformation exercises. Some may be done as a group. Others may be done individually, with group members reporting back to each other about how they heard God during the exercise.

For either type of retreat, allow plenty of time for pondering. May these studies help you move a few steps closer to living your life in union with God.

# 1

---

## BELIEVING IN
## A GOD WHO HEALS

### PSALM 103

How skilled are you at admitting you're wrong? When I was wrong in my newlywed years, I choked in my attempts to admit it. So I would say to my spouse in a cartoonish voice, "Yes, you are right, and I am wrong." It took years before I could admit mistakes in a normal tone of voice.

Why are we so reluctant to admit our errors—even to God? It probably has to do with our view of God. Belief in a forgiving, healing God provides a safe atmosphere in which to admit our sins. Our objections to admitting sin fade away.

Objection 1: *Admitting sins makes us feel like failures.*

Truth: Unlike us, God is not shocked that we sin.

Objection 2: *Admitting sins makes me feel as if God is mad at me.*

Truth: The scope of God's grace is nothing short of astonishing. God is so compassionate we cannot imagine it.

## Turning Toward God

How would you verbalize our objections to confessing sin?

## Hearing God Through the Word

Psalm 103 is ordinarily thought of as a cheery psalm about blessing God. But if you track the references to sins, iniquities, transgressions and healing (vv. 9-12), you see that it also has confessional aspects. To this psalmist, however, confession was not about beating himself up but about recounting God's goodness. God is not shocked that we are fragile, sinful creatures. God is eager to forgive and heal.

*"To confess your sins to God is not to tell him anything he doesn't already know. Until you confess them, however, they are the abyss between you. When you confess them, they become the Golden Gate bridge."*

FREDERICK
BUECHNER

*Read Psalm 103:1-5.*

1. What "benefits" of God does the psalmist long to remember?

2. What does the psalmist tell himself not to do regarding God's benefits? Why might those examining their soul and "inmost being" be prone to do this?

*Read Psalm 103:6-13.*

3. Verse 6 has been dubbed a definition of God's anger,

indicating that God shows anger not in meanness or intimidation but with straightforward consequences for wrongs done. What other clues to the character of God's anger does this passage offer?

4. What good news do these verses have for people conscious of their sins and willing to confess them?

5. Find the three illustrations of how vast God's love is in verses 11-13.

*"Humility allows us to be real. We no longer have to put on a good face or false front. There is no need to impress or to hide. We are not trying to protect or advance ourselves in God's eyes."*

**MARJORIE THOMPSON**

**Read Psalm 103:14-18.**

6. What images are used to describe the frailty of humans?

7. Why is it helpful for people confessing sin to be mindful of the frailty of humans, even those who love God passionately?

8. How does remembering that I am like dust or a blown-away flower help me be more compassionate to others?

9. Fearing God is mentioned three times ("those who fear him," vv. 11, 13, 17), but look at the words around this phrase. What does appropriate fear of God involve?

*"God becomes the constant examiner of your soul, but His exams are not shameful, painful events. You're eager to follow God's ways, so the 'repentance is sweet,' and confession of sin brings love and tranquillity."*

JEANNE GUYON

**Read Psalm 103:19-22.**

10. What does the psalmist say is the proper response to such a compassionate, benevolent God?

11. What does it teach us about confession of sin to see how this confessional psalm stays focused on God and the goodness of God?

12. How would a regular habit of reflection and confession build your trust in God's love for you?

## Transformation Exercises

Experiment with one or more of the following.

• Pick a word or phrase from this passage (perhaps, "heals all your diseases" or "as far as the east is from the west, so far has he removed our transgressions from us"). For several minutes, sit or stand in that phrase. Don't think about anything much, except the grandness of God who loves you. Respond with a gesture, movement or facial expression.

• Imagine God's face of disappointment and tears as God forgives your sin and heals you. Based on what you know of God in Scripture, what might God say to you?

• Hold an object in your hand that symbolizes a wrong you've done—a wooden spoon you used to spank your child in anger, the key to a car you drove as you treated another driver with contempt, an article of clothing you wore to attract someone inappropriately. As you hold it, read Psalm 103:8-10, and try to confess aloud to God what you did. Then toss the object aside and read aloud verses 11-13.

# 2

## LETTING GOD
## SEARCH MY HEART

I CORINTHIANS 13:1-7

For many years I confessed my sins to God by scanning a long checklist of possible sins. If nothing else popped out at me, I could count on having to confess laziness and grouchiness. I'd leave my confession time hoping I'd felt guilty enough to shape up.

But shaming myself did not help me grow in God. It just made me a guilt-drenched, navel-gazing Christian. I was spiritually self-absorbed—a condition that contradicts everything in Christianity. I see now that I was taking the wrong thing seriously: my supposed righteousness. What I needed to take seriously was God's grace and desire to live in me. God would change me as we interacted, not as I shamed myself.

In interaction with God, we hear God's voice of gentle correction especially when we're serving others (what attitudes I have!) and when we're reading and meditating on Scripture. In such moments

God probes our hearts, helping us see what causes us to offer hurtful innuendo, to ignore people, to pretend to be better than we are.

In the last session we saw that the foundation of confession is a belief in God's radical love for us. This frees us to examine feelings, questions, observations, suspicions, beliefs and commitments in the safety of this interactive life. The Holy Spirit helps us: "The lamp of the LORD searches the spirit of a man; it searches out his inmost being" (Proverbs 20:27). In this we find the liberty to stop beating ourselves up.

## Turning Toward God

God often seems to ask us to look at our behavior and see how we fall short. What do we do instead?

## Hearing God Through the Word

*Read 1 Corinthians 13:1-3.*

1. What remarkable gifts, qualities or actions are named in this passage that people can do but still have no love in them?

   How is it possible to do such admired, heroic actions without love?

*Read 1 Corinthians 13:4-7.*

2. Read 1 Corinthians 13:4-7 a second time, replacing the words *love* and *it* with *God*. Which of the qualities of God below do you admire most, desiring to incorporate them into your life?

| | | |
|---|---|---|
| God is patient. | God is kind. | God does not envy. |
| God does not boast. | God is not proud. | God is not rude. |
| God is not self-seeking. | God is not easily angered. | God keeps no record of wrongs. |
| God always hopes. | God always protects. | God always trusts. |
| God does not delight in evil but rejoices with the truth. | God always perseveres. | God never fails. |

*"Lay your entire soul open before God. You can be sure the Lord will not fail to enlighten you concerning your sin. Your Lord will shine as a light in you; and through His shining, He will allow you to see the nature of all your faults."*

JEANNE GUYON

3. Close your eyes, and ask God to show you whatever you need to know about yourself in light of this passage. Don't beat yourself up. Stay out of the way, and see what comes to you.

4. What are some common statements about God that make it sound as if God is rude, self-seeking or easily angered?

5. Notice the other activity of love (and of God) listed in verse 5. How could we imitate God in this way and treat ourselves more graciously?

6. What do these verses tell us about the process of self-reflection?

   • "Let us examine our ways and test them, and let us return to the LORD" (Lamentations 3:40).

   • "If we claim to be without sin, we deceive ourselves and the truth is not in us. If we confess our sins, he is faithful and just and will forgive us our sins and purify us from all unrighteousness" (1 John 1:8-9).

   • "Examine yourselves to see whether you are in the faith; test yourselves" (2 Corinthians 13:5).

   • "So then, each of us will give an account of himself to God" (Romans 14:12).

---

7. Reflection is about posing questions to oneself. What are some helpful questions to ask when examining yourself?

> *"Self-examination is not an invitation to psychoanalysis, problem solving, self-lecturing, or ego-absorption. The whole point of self-examination is to become more God-centered by observing the moments when we are or are not so."*
>
> MARJORIE
> THOMPSON

---

8. Where does the process of reflection most often break down for you?

   __ I don't ask myself reflective questions because it's too scary.

___ I don't ask myself reflective questions because it's too much work.

___ I don't ask myself reflective questions because I believe in thinking positively.

___ I don't ask myself reflective questions because I don't want to know my real motives and my real self.

___ Other:

_____

9. What do you need to believe deeply about God in order to examine your real self and your real motives without beating yourself up?

_____

10. What traps do you fall into during reflection?

___ being blind to my character flaws

___ making excuses for wrong behavior

___ berating myself, hoping that feelings of shame will force me to improve

___ letting self-examination be a onetime event

___ evaluating myself on my own power and not relying on the Spirit to search me

___ being surprised (and even horrified) that I've failed again

___ keeping the focus on me and how I'm not good enough

___ other:

*"Real damage comes when we indict ourselves for misdeeds far more vindictively than any of our friends—or God—ever would. [Healthy] guilt feels like a simple recognition of a truth in the presence of someone lovingly forgiving us."*

TAD DUNNE

11. How does a clear-eyed recognition of our faults help us choose which spiritual disciplines can help us most?

# Transformation Exercises

Experiment with one or more of the following.

- When you catch yourself in a moment of lust, pride, greed or envy, ask God to reveal to you the neediness in your heart that causes this sin.

- Before going to sleep, review your day and confess thoughts and deeds that were not motivated by love. Don't drift off to sleep until you have rested in God's love.

- Sit in a swing or bath, or perch somewhere with a pleasant view. Review the events of your past week. Look at specific events and ask yourself, *Was I motivated by God's love, or was there something else I was loving and pursuing instead?*

- Journal about how safe or unsafe you feel in giving the Holy Spirit official permission to probe you and show you what needs to be revealed to you.

- Read Colossians 3:1-12, and notice how people who had been "raised with Christ" are encouraged to put off certain qualities and put on others. Then read the how-to instructions in verses 13-17. What phrase in this passage speaks to you?

# 3

## CONFESSING TO GOD

PSALM 51

For years I attended a support group in which we reflected on our behavior in light of what we were learning about more healthy ways to respond to life. During the first few sessions I hung my head as I confessed, looking at the floor and covering my face with my hands. I dreaded looking up. But I soon learned that when I looked up, I would see nodding, smiling faces of people who accepted me. Thus I found the group to be a safe place to confess my latest mistakes and even my deeper character flaws. This experience provided me with a powerful picture of how God receives our confessions with unfailing love.

If we have a clear-eyed view of God's full-hearted compassion, admitting our wrongs to God can be one of our great moments of connection with God. This session's passage shows us a confessing sinner who did not run away from God but ran to safety in the refuge of God's arms.

This image of running to safety can help convince us that the purpose of confession is not to feel beaten up and overwhelmed. The purpose is always to love God more and be more enthralled with the great God who loves us. Confessing is not about destructive introspection or morbid brooding on failures. It brings freedom and all sorts of benefits, including transparency with God and with others. Coming clean this way helps us accept our weaknesses as well as strengths, our brokenness as well as giftedness.

## Turning Toward God

If you were to imagine God in the form of a person, what gesture or facial expression would indicate God's willingness to forgive and restore?

## Hearing God Through the Word

The confessing sinner in Psalm 51 is Israel's greatest king, David. His misdeeds began with adultery with Bathsheba, after which he murdered her husband Uriah to cover up the deed. His sin affected the entire nation and stained the name of God with scandal. This "man after [God's] own heart" (Acts 13:22) lived in self-delusion for almost a year. After being confronted, he confessed.

*"We are inviting the Lord to search our hearts to the depths. Far from being dreadful, this is a scrutiny of love."*

RICHARD FOSTER

*Read Psalm 51:1, as well as the introductory sentence to the psalm.*

1. On what truth does David base his plea for pardon?

2.  What does this verse say to people who have sinned so grievously that they feel God can't forgive them?

**Read Psalm 51:2-5.**

3.  What phrases indicate David's frankness about his sin?

4.  How does such transparency train us to be authentic people?

5.  Why do you think David emphasizes that his sin was against God, even saying, "Against you, you only, have I sinned" (v. 4)?

**Read Psalm 51:6-15.**

6.  What phrases describe the way forward into restoration?

*"Once you have established a relationship with your Lord, you will soon discover that no fault in you escapes the reproof of God. As soon as you commit a sin, you are immediately rebuked by an inward sense. It will be a kind of deep, inward burning . . . a tender confusion. He will not allow any sin to be hidden or concealed."*

JEANNE GUYON

7. What sorts of things does David pray for in his prayer of renewal (vv. 12-15)?

**Read Psalm 51:16-19.**

8. What prevents us from having a broken and contrite heart?

9. What are the chief benefits of admitting our sins to God?

*"Confession unlocks a process of spiritual healing, opening us to forgiveness, cleansing, reconciliation and renewal."*

MARJORIE THOMPSON

10. What negative character qualities might be slowly overcome as we practice this discipline of confessing to God?

11. How might confession build humility?

How might it build courage?

# Transformation Exercises

Experiment with one or more of the following.

- Reread Psalm 51 aloud slowly. Which word or phrase is most meaningful to you? Why? What does that phrase tell you about how you want to connect with God?

- Picture or draw an image to represent how God receives our confessions (such as my mental image of the nodding face of another support group member).

- Go for a walk and pause. Pick up a rock and hold it gently in your hand. Name it after a sin you've committed. Lift it up and offer it to God. Sit in silence for several minutes. Then respond however God leads you to respond.

- Figure out something you could say to a friend or acquaintance that would allow you to be more transparent than you've ever been before. Pray and ask God if you should say it.

- Find a song that expresses your sorrow for your sin ("Dear Lord and Father of Mankind," "Create in Me a Clean Heart, O God," "There Is a Balm in Gilead"). Sing it to God after acknowledging a sin.

# 4

## COMING CLEAN
## TO OTHERS

### 2 SAMUEL 11:22—12:14

To many people, admitting one's sins to another person seems unnecessary. As long as you confess to God, the issue is taken care of, right? Yet Scripture provides examples and instructions for acknowledging sins to a spiritual adviser or to others. The crowds confessed to John the Baptist in the wilderness (Matthew 3:6). The new Ephesian believers confessed their evil deeds to Paul (Acts 19:18).

The assumption that confessing only to God is always enough is a reflection of the individualistic mindset inherent in Western culture. Since the beginning of the church, confession to others has been practiced widely. When early-twentieth-century Canadian missionary Jonathan Goforth preached throughout China, it was not unusual for Christians to confess their sins publicly for several hours. The result was that the townspeople saw a tremendous change in these

Christians, came to the meetings and became Christians themselves.[*]

Many advantages come to those who unburden themselves to another person. "He who conceals his sins does not prosper, but whoever confesses and renounces them finds mercy" (Proverbs 28:13). Confession, followed by prayer, facilitates healing: "Therefore confess your sins to each other and pray for each other so that you may be healed. The prayer of a righteous man is powerful and effective" (James 5:16). We are all a "chosen race, a royal priesthood" with a ministry of reconciliation, equipping us to receive each other's confessions (1 Peter 2:9; 2 Corinthians 5:20).

Being open and honest about our mistakes facilitates true community, which isn't just about people agreeing and affirming each other. It's also about people who have reason to hate each other choosing to love instead.

## Turning Toward God

What is (or would be) the most difficult aspect of admitting your sin to another person?

• embarrassment

• finding the right words

• finding someone I could trust enough to confess to

• other:

---

[*]Illustrations abound in every chapter of Jonathan Goforth, *By My Spirit* (Minneapolis: Bethany Fellowship, 1964).

# Hearing God Through the Word

King David, whom we encountered in the last session, confessed not only to God but to his spiritual adviser, Nathan. After Nathan confronted him, David could have made excuses or railed or even had Nathan executed. Instead he said words many of us find difficult to say: "Yes, I am wrong. You are right."

*Read 2 Samuel 11:22-27.*

1. Describe David's mindset upon hearing of the death of his brave warrior Uriah (whom he had murdered).

*Read 2 Samuel 12:1-6.*

2. What method did Nathan use to confront David?

3. When, if ever, has God used one of these methods or approaches to help you see yourself?

   • you observe a situation parallel to one you're experiencing

   • you observe someone whose attitude is as bad as yours

   • a story told by a wise person

   • the words of a person who has been a positive influence in your life

• you see that you're like a person you hotly con-
demned

• other (perhaps not used in 2 Samuel 12):

*Read 2 Samuel 12:7-14.*

4. What phrases in verses 7-9, spoken by Nathan from
the viewpoint of God, communicate the heartbreak of
God over David's sin?

*"The more
isolated a person
is, the more
destructive will be
the power of sin
over him."*

DIETRICH
BONHOEFFER

5. Why were such severe consequences in order for this
esteemed man (vv. 10-12)?

6. What difference does it make that David made a dis-
tinct confession: "I have sinned against the LORD"
(v. 13)?

7. How do you explain that even though God forgave
David, David still had to experience consequences?

8. In this case, God provided Nathan's story to help David face his hidden sin. What sorts of people are open to letting God use the Holy Spirit to help them face their unrecognized or hidden sin?

9. If someone were to confess a sin to you, how—ideally—could you respond with grace and gravity?

*"In the confession of concrete sins the old man dies a painful, shameful death before the eyes of the brother. . . . In confession the break-through to new life occurs."*

DIETRICH BONHOEFFER

10. When is it helpful to confess to a person you sinned against?

11. How might admitting sin to others—whenever you become conscious of it—change your character?

  __ moving from pride to humility

  __ moving from fear to courage

  __ moving from apathy to charity

  __ moving from deceitfulness to honesty

  __ moving from turmoil to peace

  __ other:

12. What is the next step for you?

    __ asking God's forgiveness for sin

    __ finding someone to confess to because you have something to confess

    __ confessing simply: There is a sin that I cannot bring myself to confess. Pray for me.

    __ confessing to the person you have sinned against

    __ asking God to show you the next step because you have no idea

    __ other:

## Transformation Exercises

Experiment with one or more of the following.

- Reread Psalm 51 and note how far David had moved from his hardened heart evident in 2 Samuel 11:27.

- Try writing out a confession of a sin you have committed. Ask God to show you who might be a wise, trustworthy person to whom you could reveal it. Be patient in waiting to hear. (You also have the option of tearing it up as a sign of God's forgiveness.)

- Make a list of situations that have annoyed you recently. Then take a walk and ask God to "connect the dots" between those situations and the sinful behaviors you do habitually. Don't try too hard. Just walk.

- Look at someone you love and say, "You are right, and I am wrong." How does it feel? In what matter is it usually true that you are wrong and this person is right?

# 5

---

# RECOGNIZING
# GOD'S PRESENCE
# IN MY LIFE

PSALM 65:1-13

In movies, country folk often say, "Well, I recollect . . ." and they tell you what they remember. Many sentences in Scripture begin with "Remember," because we need to recollect how we have experienced God. Not all of these experiences happen at church. We can be drawn to God while reading a letter, holding a memento or glancing at the sky before getting into a car in a parking lot. Recollecting these moments is another facet of reflection and confession. We take time to acknowledge how God is speaking to us in our lives.

This process of recollection is part of what has been called the "prayer of examen," a prayer pattern used for centuries by Christians. It has two parts—the examination of *conscience* and the examination of *consciousness*. In the former we search for wrongs done and admit them (sessions 2-4). In the latter we gently search our lives for divine moments. We ask ourselves questions such as these:

- Did I meet God in the joy or pain of others?

- Did I bring Christ into my world in some way?

- Did anyone bring God to me?

- Did I reach out to someone in trouble or sorrow?

- Did I fail or refuse to do so?

- Did something that happened to me today give me a keener sense of being loved, or being angry or tired, or needing God in some special way?

- Is there any concrete event of the day that revealed some part of my life that I am withholding from God?

Prayers of examen change our way of seeing and become a rhythm of life. In fact, many use such prayers every evening, while others use them once a week or month or year. They enlighten us to the brilliant hues of our connection with God.

## Turning Toward God

What is the best thing that has happened to you recently?

## Hearing God Through the Word

The writer of Psalm 65 seems to have had many moments of experiencing God. In this thanksgiving psalm, he speaks directly to God, recalling, reflecting and recollecting how God has forgiven, worked in power and provided.

***Read Psalm 65:1-4.***

---

1. Even though the psalmist was at one time overwhelmed by sin (v. 3), what is his state now?

---

2. In prayers of reflection and confession, why is it important to include expressions of what we intend to do to change our ways (such as the psalmist's vows mentioned in v. 1)?

---

3. Think of something you've done recently that you're not proud of. What is the way forward from that behavior? As you answer, don't mention the wrong deed, but begin your answer by saying, "Learning to . . ."

***Read Psalm 65:5-8.***

---

4. How did God answer the psalmist's prayer?

---

5. What are some ways you have recently experienced "answers" from God?

___ something good or right happened ("deeds of righteousness," v. 5)

___ God's power created a new outward circumstance or inner condition in you or someone else ("armed yourself with strength," v. 6)

___ God's power stilled a troublesome circumstance or inner condition in you or someone else or even in a nation ("stilled the roaring," v. 7)

___ those living far away saw God at work (v. 8)

___ other:

_____

6. What are some simple ways we can recollect with "songs of joy" when "morning dawns and evening fades?"

*"God invites us to discern the footprints of the Holy, to rehearse the mighty deeds of God."*

RICHARD FOSTER

_____

7. When do you regularly reflect on what God has done in your life? (If you don't, when might you like to?)

**Read Psalm 65:9-13.**

_____

8. How did the psalmist experience God's intervening in his life and providing?

9. What are the "grasslands" and "meadows" in your life that have sprouted in the past year?

in the past week?

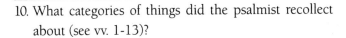

10. What categories of things did the psalmist recollect about (see vv. 1-13)?

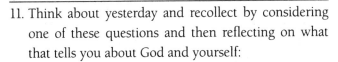

11. Think about yesterday and recollect by considering one of these questions and then reflecting on what that tells you about God and yourself:

- What surprised me?
- What touched or moved me?
- What encounters nurtured me?

*"If we pray the Examen regularly, generously, and courageously, . . . we will begin to see ourselves and understand our actions in a whole new way. We will begin to recognize God in all things, to rejoice in the invitational, relational love of God."*

DEBORAH SMITH
DOUGLAS

12. How might a discipline of recollection lead to development of disciplines of practicing the presence of God and worshiping throughout the day?

# Transformation Exercises

Experiment with one or more of the following.

- At the end of a day, consider two or three of the questions in question 11.

- Compare the elements of the prayer of examen of conscience developed by Ignatius Loyola (below) with the elements in Psalm 65. How many are similar?

    give thanks to God for benefits received

    ask grace to know my sins and rid myself of them

    account for my soul from the hour of rising to the present moment

    ask God's pardon for faults

    resolve with God's grace to amend them (How can I change? What is the way forward?)

- Pray, asking God to help you notice the "answers" from God listed in question 5 for the next three days.

# 6

## JOURNALING

JEREMIAH 15:10-21; 17:5-8

A help to me in working things out has been to keep an honest . . . unpublishable journal. . . . Not long ago someone I love said something which wounded me grievously. So, in great pain, I crawled to my journal and wrote it all out in a great burst of self-pity. And when I had set it down, I saw that something I myself had said had called forth the words which had hurt me so. It had, in fact, been my own fault. But I would never have seen it if I had not written it out.

In the quote above Madeleine L'Engle describes the revelatory nature of a journal written with God as the audience. As we put experiences and feelings into concrete words, we create an opportunity for God to speak to us. The point of journaling is to reveal the inner workings of our hearts with complete honesty so we see ourselves and our behavior more clearly. That's why a journal is an ideal place to admit our sins or sort out what we need to say to God.

A journal also invites us to explore issues of neediness behind our sin: *why am I so angry?* Journaling must not, however, degenerate into spiritual navel gazing; it's merely another way to connect with God. If writing words seems too tedious for you, you can jog or ride a bike or do stitchery and release thoughts to God in a similar way. We focus our bodies on an activity while pondering before God in a less formal way.

## Turning Toward God

Which of these concerns might keep you from journaling?

- worry that someone will read the journal

- feeling that it's too painful to go over a conflict

- disliking to write things down (a friend of mine is so intimidated by the idea of journaling that she insists she merely "scribbles" now and then)

- feeling obligated to write in it every day (actually you can journal once a week, once a month or whenever you need to)

- thinking you need to have a special sort of book (really a spiral notebook or a computer will do)

- other:

# Hearing God Through the Word

In a journal-like fashion, the prophet Jeremiah recorded confessions, laments, monologues, dialogues and disputes with God. Called as a boy to preach doom and destruction, Jeremiah was asked to remain celibate (Jeremiah 16:1-3). He was shunned by friends, plotted against by residents of his hometown (11:18-19) and put in a cistern by government officials (38:1-6). You can see why he processed so much grief before God!

*Read Jeremiah 15:10-14.*

1. What was Jeremiah's complaint?

*"I have been keeping these notebooks of thoughts and questions and sometimes just garbage (which needs to be dumped somewhere) since I was about nine, and they are, I think, my free psychiatrist's couch."*

MADELEINE
L'ENGLE

2. Jeremiah's despair stemmed from his interactions with God, recorded in chapters 14—15.

| Jeremiah's Request | God's Reply |
|---|---|
| asked for relief from the drought (14:1-9) | did not agree to send rain (14:10-12) |
| interceded for Judah by saying that their prophets had misled them (14:13) | agreed with Jeremiah, but continued to condemn the people of Judah (14:14-18) |
| acknowledged Judah's guilt but asked for mercy (14:19-22) | did not relent about sending Judah into captivity (15:1-9) |

When have you gotten "no" answers from God and felt discouraged as Jeremiah did?

*Read Jeremiah 15:15-18.*

3. What truths about the character of God does Jeremiah
   state (vv. 15-18)?

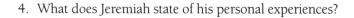

4. What does Jeremiah state of his personal experiences?

5. What does Jeremiah state of his feelings?

*"In journaling,
we know
ourselves as we
really are and feel
the acceptance of
the one who loves
us without
reservation."*

ANNE BROYLES

6. What questions does Jeremiah ask?

7. If you were to write in a journal, which of the following elements of Jeremiah's lament would you probably
   include?

   __ complaints

   __ reminding yourself about the character of God

   __ personal experiences

   __ feelings

   __ questions you want to ask God

   __ other:

***Read Jeremiah 15:19-21.***

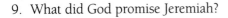

8. What did God want of Jeremiah?

9. What did God promise Jeremiah?

10. How do you think God "answers" people as they journal?

***Read Jeremiah 17:5-8.***

11. How did God later describe the person who is cursed and the one who is blessed?

12. Why would it be easier to confess to God in a journal than aloud to God or to another person?

Why would it be more difficult?

*"I confess,
O God—
that often I let
my mind wander
down unclean
and forbidden
ways; . . .
that often, by
concealing my
real motives, I
pretend to be
better than I am;
that often my
affection for my
friends is only a
refined form of
caring for myself;
that often I do
good deeds only
that they may be
seen of men, and
shun evil ones
only because I
fear they may be
found out.
O holy One, let
the fire of Thy love
enter my heart,
and burn up all
this coil of
meanness and
hypocrisy, and
make my heart as
the heart of a little
child."*

JOHN BAILLIE

# Transformation Exercises

Experiment with one or more of the following.

- Journal or draw or record your thoughts on a tape or CD about a complaint, a personal experience or a feeling. Be alert to anything you need to confess, questions you need to ask or characteristics of God you need to remind yourself of. (Any time you journal, feel free to tear it up when you're finished, if you need to do so.)

- Think of a resentment you feel and work through the following questions in a journal.

    Examine the cause—how did this resentment occur?

    What have been the effects of this resentment on you (withdrawal, defensiveness, fear of rejection, need to prove self, isolation, repressed anger, approval seeking, control, caretaking, fear of abandonment, fear of authority figures, frozen feelings, over- or underdeveloped sense of responsibility)?

    What was your part, if any, in bringing this resentment or its effects upon you?

    If you would like freedom from this resentment, confess it to God and ask God to help you be delivered from it.

- Draw something or play an instrument, and notice how such activities can resemble journaling. What do you learn from the songs you choose to sing or the objects you choose to draw? What could you sing or draw that would serve as a confession for you?

# GUIDELINES FOR LEADERS

*My grace is sufficient for you.* *(2 Corinthians 12:9)*

If leading a small group is something new for you, don't worry. These sessions are designed to be led easily. Because the Bible study questions flow from observation to interpretation to application, you may feel as if the studies lead themselves.

You don't need to be an expert on the Bible or a trained teacher to lead a small group discussion. As a leader, you can guide group members to discover for themselves what the Bible has to say and to listen for God's guidance. This method of learning will allow group members to remember much more of what is said than a lecture would.

This study guide is flexible. You can use it with a variety of groups—students, professionals, neighborhood or church folks. Each study takes forty-five to sixty minutes in a group setting.

It's true that getting people to discuss the Bible requires some thought. The suggestions listed below will help you encourage discussion by paying attention to group dynamics.

## Preparing for the Study

1. Ask God to help you understand and apply the passage in your own life. Unless this happens, you will not be prepared to lead others. Pray too for the various members of the group. Ask God to open your hearts to the message and motivate you to action.

2. Read the introduction to the entire guide to get an overview of the issues that will be explored.

3. As you begin each study, read and reread the assigned Scripture passage to familiarize yourself with it. Read also the focus statement at the beginning of the notes for that study, which appear later in this section.

4. This study guide is based on the New International Version of the Bible. It will help you and the group if you use this translation as the basis for your study and discussion.

5. Carefully work through each question in the study. Spend time in meditation and reflection as you consider how to respond.

6. Write your thoughts and responses in the space provided in the study guide. This will help you to express your understanding of the passage clearly.

7. It may help to have a Bible dictionary handy. Use it to look up any unfamiliar words, names or places. (For additional help on how to study a passage, see *How to Lead a LifeGuide Bible Study* from InterVarsity Press.)

8. Consider how you need to apply the Scripture to your life. Remember that the group members will follow your lead in responding to the studies. They will not go any deeper than you do.

## Leading the Study

1. Begin the study on time. Open with prayer, asking God to help the group to understand and apply the passage.

2. Be sure that everyone in your group has a study guide. There are some questions and activities they will need to work through on their own before, during or after the study session.

3. At the beginning of your first session together, explain that these studies are meant to be discussions, not lectures. Encourage the members of the group to participate. However, do not put pressure on those who may be hesitant to speak during the first few sessions. You may want to suggest

the following guidelines to your group.

- Stick to the topic being discussed.

- Base your response on the verses studied, not on outside authorities such as commentaries or speakers.

- Focus on the passage of Scripture studied. Only rarely should you refer to other portions of the Bible. This allows for everyone to participate on equal ground and for in-depth study.

- Anything said in the group is considered confidential and will not be discussed outside the group unless specific permission is given to do so.

- Help everyone get involved by limiting your responses if you contribute a lot or by responding more if you're usually quiet. But don't feel forced to speak up.

- Listen attentively to each other and learn from one another.

- Pray for each other, especially if you feel that someone is struggling with an answer. Praying is better than interrupting.

4. Have a group member read aloud the introduction at the beginning of the discussion.

5. Every session begins with a "Turning Toward God" section. The questions or activities are meant to be used before the passage is read. These questions introduce the theme of the study and encourage group members to begin to open up. Encourage as many members as possible to participate, and be ready to get the discussion going with your own response.

6. Have one or more group member(s) read aloud the passage to be studied.

7. As you ask the questions under "Hearing God Through the Word," keep in mind that they are designed to be used just as they are written. You may simply read them aloud. Or you may prefer to express them in your own words.

There may be times when it is appropriate to deviate from the study guide. For example, a question may have already been answered. If so, move on to the next question. Or someone may raise an important question not covered in the guide. Take time to discuss it, but try to keep the group from going off on tangents.

8. Avoid answering your own questions. If necessary repeat or rephrase them until they are clearly understood. Or point out something you read in the leader's notes to clarify the context or meaning. An eager group quickly becomes passive and silent if members think the leader will do most of the talking.

9. Don't be afraid of silence in response to the discussion questions. People may need time to think about the question before formulating their answers. Count to twenty before rephrasing or commenting.

10. Don't be content with just one answer. Ask, "What do the rest of you think?" or "Anything else?" until several people have given answers to the question.

11. Acknowledge all contributions. Try to be affirming whenever possible. Never reject an answer. If it is clearly off-base, ask, "Which verse led you to that conclusion?" or again, "What do the rest of you think?"

12. Don't expect every answer to be addressed to you, even though this will probably happen at first. As group members become more at ease, they will begin to truly interact with each other. This is one sign of healthy discussion.

13. Don't be afraid of controversy. It can be very stimulating. If you don't resolve an issue completely, don't be frustrated. Explain that the group will move on and God may enlighten group members in later sessions.

14. Periodically summarize what the group has said about the passage. This helps to draw together the various ideas mentioned and gives continuity to the study. But don't preach.

15. Every session ends with "Transformation Exercises." At the end of the study, have a participant read them aloud. Then ask each participant to choose the one that fits them best, according to their personality or current needs. Ask them to tell the group which one that is and a time they could try it.

    Before the next session starts, ask whether any participants tried the transformation exercises. You might lead into this by telling about one you tried. So-called failures really are not failures. These things are a matter of skill building. You never learn to ride a bike unless you get on it the first time and keep trying.

16. Conclude your time together with conversational prayer, adapting the prayer suggestion at the end of the study to your group. Ask for God's help in following through on the commitments you've made.

17. End on time.

Many more suggestions and helps can be found in *The Big Book on Small Groups* (from InterVarsity Press).

# STUDY NOTES

## Session 1. Believing in a God Who Heals
### *Psalm 103*

*Focus:* Even when confessing sin, we bask in the love and compassion of our almighty God.

**Turning Toward God.** Bring up images of people sitting under bare lightbulbs in military prisons and in back rooms of organized crime. More benignly, confessing reminds us of our failures.

**Question 1.** "Healing" diseases (v. 3) is more than "merely bodily diseases, but all kinds of inward and outward sufferings."[1] Also, the parallelism of Hebrew poetry, as in verse 3 (two parallel lines offering the same meaning with different words), shows that to be forgiven is to find healing.

**Question 3.** The word for *accuse* (v. 9) was used in a legal sense and does not refer to harping or nagging or being mean. God also does not "harbor anger," indulging it or brooding. God's anger is "not carried to the full extent" of what it could be, considering God's power.[2] God's justice or anger is not measured out according to what we have done but according to what God believes is right. God is not about "payback" (v. 10).

---

[1]Franz Delitzsch, *Commentary on the Old Testament,* vol. 5, *Commentary on the Psalms* (Grand Rapids, Mich.: Eerdmans, 1973), p. 120.
[2]Ibid., p. 122.

**Question 5.** As vast as the distance from heaven to earth, as vast as the distance from east to west, as immense as a father's love for his child.

**Question 6.** Dust and "grass, which in the dry Orient is often of such short duration. It takes no more than the passing of the hot wind of the desert over it on certain hot days, and the grass is gone."[3]

**Question 7.** Humility comes from a realistic understanding of who we are in relation to God. Otherwise it's easy for Christians to view themselves as superior to others or "better" than they were before their life in Christ. Humility helps us understand that everything depends on Christ. Awareness of our fragility leads to an uninflated, realistic view of ourselves.

**Question 8.** Says Marjorie Thompson, "As we perceive the realities of sin in ourselves, we can identify with the brokenness of others. Instead of condemning someone whose behavior is irritating or unacceptable, we may recall similar behavior in our own lives."[4]

**Question 9.** The words for fear in Hebrew and Greek are sometimes translated as *dread* or *terror*. Other times they're translated to imply a healthy fear, even reverence. The translators seem to rely on the context, and so should we. The context in the psalm points to a compassionate, merciful God. This makes it clear that the fear mentioned here is not dread or terror but a holy, wholesome fear of disappointing or grieving the great God we love and are devoted to. God does not delight in terrifying folks but in finding a contrite, willing heart within them.

**Question 11.** The purpose of confession is not to feel beaten up and overwhelmed. The purpose is always to love God more and be more enthralled with the great God who loves us. We are limited, finite followers of God, being slowly transformed into Christlikeness.

---

[3]H. C. Leupold, *Exposition of the Psalms* (Grand Rapids, Mich.: Baker, 1972), 1:719-20.
[4]Marjorie Thompson, *Soul Feast* (Louisville, Ky.: Westminster John Knox, 1995), p. 98.

## Session 2. Letting God Search My Heart
### 1 Corinthians 13:1-7

*Focus:* We can experiment with the process of asking God to show us where our hearts lack love, confessing that lack and reestablishing ourselves in God's love.

**Question 1.** An eloquent speaker, a person with prophetic power, an especially wise person, someone whose faith everyone trusts, a donor who gives up the rest of his fortune, a martyr. The heart is so deceitful that people can do good (even devout) deeds without a heart of love. "The heart is deceitful above all things and beyond cure. Who can understand it?" (Jeremiah 17:9). Think of it—Paul was worried about martyrs dying with hearts of self-righteousness. We'd figure, "Gee, they're martyrs! They must be pure no matter what's in their heart!"

**Question 2.** After reading the passage the second time, explain that reading this convicting passage this way will help us avoid the sin of emphasizing human flaws rather than being enthralled with the great God who loves us. Confession is to be grounded in the self-giving love of God.

**Question 3.** Read the Marjorie Thompson quotation on page 19 before reading question 3 (p. 18). Allow three to five minutes of silence for this. Gently end the silence with a quiet prayer, thanking God that God speaks to us, and asking God to keep speaking and prodding us about whatever we need to know about ourselves.

**Question 5.** Because God "keeps no record of wrongs," we need to do the same for ourselves (after we've confessed and asked for forgiveness). By focusing on our mistakes and faults, we are focusing on or "delighting in evil," instead of rejoicing in the truth that God's power is transforming us (v. 6). God's love moves us forward instead of beating us back.

**Question 7.** You may wish to suggest this question about any situation:

Was I motivated by God's love, or was there something else I was loving and pursuing instead?

**Question 10.** *Berating myself, hoping . . .* You may wish to have group participants look up these verses: "The Spirit searches all things, even the deep things of God" (1 Corinthians 2:10). "I the LORD search the heart and examine the mind, to reward a man according to his conduct, according to what his deeds deserve" (Jeremiah 17:10).

If you try to be the one who does the examining, there is a very good chance that you will deceive yourself. You will never really allow yourself to see your true state. This is the simple fact about the nature of your own self-love. "We call the evil good, and the good evil"[5] (Isaiah 5:20).

*Letting self-examination be . . .* Colossians 3:1-10 shows that even as we've been "raised with Christ," we need to continually "put to death . . . whatever belongs to [our] earthly nature" and "put on the new self, which is being renewed in knowledge in the image of its Creator."

**Question 11.** As you see your faults, you can ask God to show you which spiritual disciplines would be helpful. For example, if you discern that you are lazy, you might ask God for a spiritual discipline of service. If you see that you are angry, you might ask for a spiritual discipline of meditation (brooding on God instead of self) or fasting (not getting what I want and learning to live with that).

## Session 3. Confessing to God
### Psalm 51

*Focus:* David's confession helps us explore the subtleties and benefits of confessing to God.

**Question 1.** God's unfailing love, not any mitigating factors or minimizing of David's sin.

---

[5]Jeanne Guyon, *Experiencing the Depths of Jesus Christ* (Beaumont, Tex.: SeedSowers, 1975), p. 74.

**Question 2.** This verse shows that forgiveness is never based on how bad or not so bad the sin was, but always on God's forgiveness. To say "God can't forgive me," then, is to say that God's love is not encompassing enough. It suggests a failure on God's part.

**Question 3.** He speaks of his iniquity (v. 2, using a Hebrew word meaning "perversion and twisting of moral standards"), sin (v. 2, "divinely appointed goal has been missed") and transgressions (v. 3, "rebellion").[6] David does not minimize his sin, make excuses, speak defensively or rehearse how wrong the other people were. He doesn't say, "I'm such a successful soldier and king—I deserve some pleasure," or "I had no choice but to . . ." When he speaks of being "sinful at birth, sinful from the time my mother conceived me," he isn't making excuses but stating the fact that all sin and fall short of the mark. As exalted as he was in Israelite society, he didn't see himself as superhuman but as flesh born of flesh.

**Question 4.** We freely admit who we are, not pretending to be better than we are. Like David, we keep our sins before us (v. 3). We don't try to make our confession sound light or casual even though we're sure of God's forgiveness. What we say is who we really are.

**Question 5.** While David did also sin against Bathsheba and Uriah, he lived as the Puritans lived—as if standing before an audience of One, that is, living to God alone.[7] All sin is then against the Holy One. This is not a reason for terror but a mark of intimacy with God. It's as if we say, "Only you, O God, know who I am truly."

**Question 6.** We need renewal not just in behavior but in the "inner parts." Even though we've been "crushed," God leads us into rejoicing. God's creativity includes purifying our hearts and giving us a steadfast spirit.

---

[6]Leupold, *Exposition of the Psalms,* p. 401.
[7]Dallas Willard, *The Divine Conspiracy* (San Francisco: HarperSanFrancisco, 1998), p. 190.

**Question 7.** A restored person naturally becomes a teacher of transgressors and one who sings of God's righteousness. Formerly crushed but newly healed bones shout of the efficacy of a great God who makes diamonds out of crushed coal.

**Question 9.** We shortchange ourselves by rushing to God to ask for forgiveness without fully confessing our sins. Being silent about sin can immobilize us (Psalm 32:3-4), but confessing sin is a constructive way to deal with guilt. Instead of languishing in shame, we can (with the help of the Spirit) determine which of our character flaws was involved and ask God to show us how to further address that flaw. Confessing sin allows us to move forward (vv. 13-15) instead of being haunted by past mistakes. It also teaches us the skill of surrendering to God who is holy yet loves us.

# Session 4. Coming Clean to Others
## 2 Samuel 11:22—12:14

*Focus:* The importance, power and process of confessing our sins to others.

**Question 1.** David covered up well. He pretended to be unconcerned and feigned encouragement to Joab (2 Samuel 11:25). Wanting to continue the cover-up, he waited until a respectable time of mourning was over before marrying Uriah's widow, Bathsheba. Overall, he was "flippant and insensitive. While he grieved deeply for Saul and Abner, his rivals (2 Sam. 1; 3:31-39), he showed no grief for Uriah, a good man with strong spiritual character. Why? . . . Deliberate, repeated sinning had dulled David's sensitivity to God's laws and others' rights. The more you try to cover up a sin, the more insensitive you become toward it."[8]

**Question 2.** Nathan used a story, which drew David in rather than causing him to be defensive. The story was about sheep owning, and David's first occupation had been to herd sheep. Nathan's details are keen: The poor man has

---

[8]*Life Application Bible* (Wheaton, Ill.: Tyndale House, 1991), p. 511.

not inherited or been given this lamb but has gone out of his way to purchase it. This creates a huge contrast between the poor man and the wealthy rancher.

**Question 4.** "I anointed . . . I delivered . . . I gave . . . I gave . . . I would have given": God communicated all he had done for David. (Verse 8 is the only mention in Scripture that David had received all of Saul's household and wives. This seems to mitigate any reason for adultery.)

"Despise the word of the LORD by doing what was evil in his eyes" tells us that in a relationship with God, disobedience is not impersonal. It's an affront to the God we have devoted ourselves to.

**Question 5.** David was a public figure with God's hand on him. For God to have overlooked this sin or to let him off lightly would have encouraged all kinds of sin in others. Often the sin of a public figure gives permission to people (even that person's children) to stop persevering against sin. The fallout is enormous. "David's children shared his weakness, but few demonstrated his redeeming characteristic of contriteness. In his frequent departures, David remained open to correction. Not so his sons."[9] To help group participants understand verses 10-12, mention that the results were the deaths of David's sons Amnon (2 Samuel 13:28-29), Absalom (2 Samuel 18:5, 9-15) and Adonijah (1 Kings 1:5-53, 2:13-25). Second Samuel 12:11 refers to Absalom's public seizure of the royal concubines (2 Samuel 16:22).

**Question 6.** It showed immediate and contrite repentance. He could have lashed out against Nathan. King Ahab, for example, called Elijah his "enemy" when Elijah confronted him about murdering Naboth for his vineyard (1 Kings 21:20).

**Question 7.** God offers *pardon* but, like a good parent, may still employ *consequences*. These are two different issues. Christians sometimes choose to sin because they know God will forgive them. And God does. But conse-

---

[9]Lawrence O. Richards, *The Teacher's Commentary* (Wheaton, Ill.: Victor, 1987), p. 237.

quences remain: we "set into motion events with irreversible consequences."[10] It was important that the child not survive because David
needed to receive no reward for his sin.

**Question 8.** Those well versed in listening to God in Scripture, solitude and all of life (including the "Nathans") will hear the Holy Spirit confront them.

**Question 9.** You would: take their confession seriously; not brush it off
by saying everyone has these problems; not be shocked and judge those
who confess; not try to fix them with self-help books and Scripture quot-
ing; not give advice; pray for them and encourage them without bringing
up past sin; ask them if they wish to be accountable, meaning that they
will check in to report progress and perhaps make contact when tempted.
Even when people check in with failures, they need words of grace and
empowerment.

Often it helps to say distinctly to confessing people that their sin is forgiven by God. You are reminding them of what they already know intel-
lectually but are struggling to believe in their deepest selves.

**Question 10.** Confessing to the person you sinned against can bring
healing and reconciliation. Do not confess when it will cause harm to the
other person. When in doubt, ask God for direction and then follow it. You
may want to back up and ask, "When is it not helpful?" and then move on
to this question.

# Session 5. Recognizing God's Presence in My Life
## Psalm 65:1-13

*Focus:* Recalling moments of the day when God's touch was noticed or
needed.

**Question 1.** He is well off, being "filled with the good things of your

---

[10]*Life Application Bible*, p. 512.

house." ("Your house" could be the temple or the "invisible courts of God's spiritual presence.")[11] He has even made vows, which are voluntary promises to do certain things or abstain from them.

**Question 2.** In all of the Christian life, it's important to be asking God, What is the next step? But this is especially true when we confess sin. Many confessions in Scripture identify what the way forward is and how the confessing person intends to follow it (see Psalm 51:13-19, a third of the psalm). When we are unsure of what the next step is, we need to ask God to show us what it is and perhaps talk with a wise friend.

**Question 4.** Although the exact prayer is not stated (v. 2), God's answer is clear: "awesome deeds of righteousness." Then the psalmist seems to say, "Why am I so surprised by this? After all . . ." and describes creation and how it exhibits God's qualities: hope through creation's vastness (v. 5), power and strength through forces of creation (vv. 6-7), and glory through the way those far away recognize God's greatness (v. 8).

**Question 5.** We do a lot of asking in our prayers. We need to watch for God's responses and acknowledge them.

**Question 6:** Some suggestions: Making it a point to enjoy each sunrise and sunset, even with a special prayer or song; using a prayer of recollection or thanksgiving each day.

**Question 7.** If participants feel blank, ask about such moments as at the Thanksgiving dinner table or in Communion.

**Question 10.** The psalmist recollected how God heard prayers (v. 2), forgave (v. 3), filled them with good things (v. 4), did actions of goodness (v. 5), gave hope (v. 5), exhibited qualities of power and strength (vv. 6-8) and exhibited constant care for creation (vv. 9-13).

---

[11]H. C. Leupold, *Exposition of the Psalms*, vol. 1 (Grand Rapids, Mich.: Baker, 1972), p. 474.

# Session 6. Journaling
## *Jeremiah 15:10-21; 17:5-8*

*Focus:* Journaling can help us face and confess thoughts and feelings.

**Question 1.** Jeremiah was in anguish, wishing he had not been born because his job of foretelling misery and ruin upon Judah was so unpopular and discouraging. Scholars generally interpret verse 10 to mean that Jeremiah cursed the day he was born. "His call dated from his mother's womb (1:5), and to curse the day of his birth was tantamount to a rejection of his very mission."[12] The second portion shows that he had not brought others' curses upon himself through fraudulent dealings.

Many commentators agree that Jeremiah 15:11-14 are difficult to interpret because the Hebrew words can be translated in various ways. C. F. Keil's sense of it is as follows: Those who cursed Jeremiah would eventually see Jeremiah was right. They would not be able to oppose Babylon, just as men can't break iron. Every word Jeremiah prophesied would come true—even the taking of Judah's treasures.[13]

**Read Jeremiah 15:15-18.** Ask that as the Scripture is read aloud the group count the personal pronouns—*you, your, me, my, I.* One person can read aloud (emphasizing the pronouns) while another participant counts. This is better than counting silently. Save this information for question 5.

**Question 3.** God understands us (v. 15); God is long-suffering (v. 15); God's words can be our "heart's delight" (v. 16). Jeremiah was acknowledging these truths before God, but he may have also reviewed them to remind himself since he was so discouraged.

**Question 5.** Suffering (v. 15), delight (v. 16), indignation (v. 17), unending pain (v. 18). Ask about the number of personal pronouns in the text.

---

[12]J. A. Thompson, *The Book of Jeremiah,* New International Commentary on the Old Testament (Grand Rapids, Mich.: Eerdmans, 1980), p. 392.

[13]C. F. Keil, *Commentary on the Old Testament: Jeremiah, Lamentations* (Grand Rapids, Mich.: Eerdmans, 1973), pp. 259-62.

Their abundance (twenty-four in NIV) indicate how deeply personal Jeremiah's prophetic book was (as well as his relationship with God). Some have compared his book to a journal.

**Question 6.** Note especially the question, "Will you be to me like a deceptive brook, like a spring that fails?" (v. 18). A brook was deceptive "when it went dry in summer and couldn't be depended on for water."[14]

**Question 8.** God wanted Jeremiah to repent of his hopelessness in cursing the day he was born. If group participants respond by saying that Jeremiah had a right to feel sorry for himself (see details in the paragraph before "Hearing God Through the Word"), state that God's response reflects the personal nature of a journal. The person journaling can often hear very difficult things from God that would sound too harsh if God used another person as a messenger.

**Question 10.** Reminding them of the truths of God; revealing truths about themselves as they reread what they've already written, as described by Madeleine L'Engle (quotation in this session's introduction).

**Question 11.** Note also that Jeremiah's new view (Jeremiah 17:8) answers his earlier questions about pain and wounds and doubts about God (15:18). He now has confidence instead of fear and worry: "Blessed is the man who trusts in the Lord, whose confidence is in him. He will be like a tree planted by the water that sends out its roots by the stream."

---

[14]Thompson, *Book of Jeremiah*, p. 397.

# SOURCES

## Introduction

Henri Nouwen, *Making All Things New* (San Francisco: HarperSanFrancisco, 1981), p. 66.

## Session 1

**SIDEBARS**
Frederick Buechner, *Wishful Thinking* (San Francisco: HarperSanFrancisco, 1993), p. 18.

Marjorie Thompson, *Soul Feast* (Louisville, Ky.: Westminster John Knox, 1995), p. 98.

Jeanne Guyon, *Experiencing the Depths of Jesus Christ* (Beaumont, Tex.: SeedSowers, 1975), p. 76.

## Session 2

**SIDEBARS**
Jeanne Guyon, *Experiencing the Depths of Jesus Christ* (Beaumont, Tex.: SeedSowers, 1975), p. 73.

Marjorie Thompson, *Soul Feast* (Louisville, Ky.: Westminster John Knox, 1995), p. 85.

Tad Dunne, *Spiritual Mentoring* (San Francisco: HarperSanFrancisco, 1991), pp. 99-100.

**TRANSFORMATION EXERCISES**
Adapted from ibid., pp. 97, 93.

## Session 3

**SIDEBARS**
Richard Foster, *Prayer: Finding the Heart's True Home* (San Francisco: HarperSanFrancisco, 1992), p. 29.

Jeanne Guyon, *Experiencing the Depths of Jesus Christ* (Beaumont, Tex.: SeedSowers, 1975), p. 74.

Marjorie Thompson, *Soul Feast* (Louisville, Ky.: Westminster John Knox, 1995), p. 85.

## Session 4

SIDEBARS
Dietrich Bonhoeffer, *Life Together* (New York: Harper & Row, 1954), p. 112.
Ibid., pp. 113-15.

## Session 5

INTRODUCTION
Deborah Smith Douglas, "The Examen Re-examined," *Weavings,* March/April 1995,
    p. 37.

SIDEBARS
Richard Foster, *Prayer: Finding the Heart's True Home* (San Francisco: HarperSanFran-
    cisco, 1992), p. 28.
Douglas, "Examen Re-examined," p. 36.

QUESTION ELEVEN
The questions have been adapted from a handout by retreat leader Linda Douty,
    Memphis, Tennessee.

TRANSFORMATION EXERCISES
The list of Ignatian elements comes from W. H. Longridge, *The Spiritual Exercises of
    Ignatius of Loyola* (London: A. R. Mowbray, 1950), p. 50.

## Session 6

INTRODUCTION
Madeleine L'Engle, *Walking on Water: Reflections on Faith and Art* (Wheaton, Ill.:
    Harold Shaw, 1980), p. 137.

SIDEBARS
Ibid.
Anne Broyles, "One More Door into God's Presence: Journaling as a Spiritual Disci-
    pline," *Weavings,* May/June 1987, p. 34.
John Baillie, *A Diary of Private Prayer* (London: Oxford University Press, 1956),
    p. 75.

## TRANSFORMATION EXERCISES

These steps are mentioned in Marjorie Thompson, *Soul Feast* (Louisville, Ky.: Westminster John Knox, 1995), p. 88. Similar processes are described in twelve-step
books.

For more information on Jan Johnson's
writing and speaking ministry, visit
**<www.janjohnson.org>**.
Or contact Jan at
4897 Abilene St.
Simi, CA 93063